FLORENCE

& TUSCANY

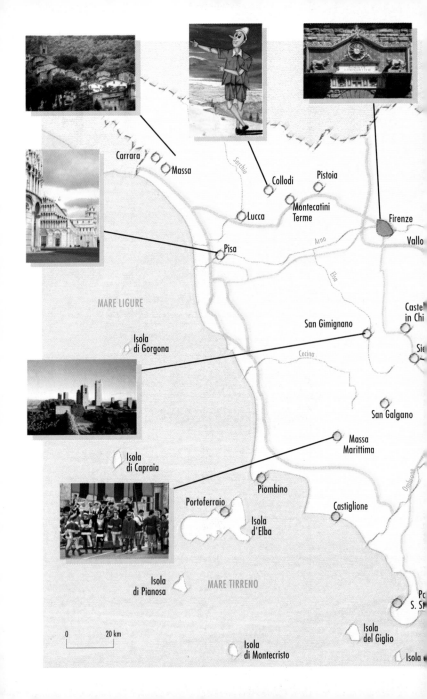

Carrara

Massa

Serchio

Collodi

Pistoia

Lucca

Montecatini
Terme

Firenze

Vallo

Pisa

Arno

Elsa

MARE LIGURE

Caste
in Chi

San Gimignano

Isola
di Gorgona

Cecina

Sie

San Galgano

Massa
Marittima

Isola
di Capraia

Ombrone

Piombino

Portoferraio

Castiglione

Isola
d'Elba

Isola
di Pianosa

MARE TIRRENO

Po
S. Si

0   20 km

Isola
del Giglio

Isola
di Montecristo

Isola

Piazza
dell'Independenza

San Ma

Galleria
dell'Accaden

Stazione centrale
di S. Maria Novella

Palazzo
Medici-Riccardi

Santa Maria
Novella

San Lorenzo

Battistero Duomo

Piazza
della
Repubblica

Orsanmichele

Bargell

Palazzo
Vecchio

Galleria
degli
Uffizi

Ponte
Vecchio

Santa Maria
del Carmine

Arno

Palazzo
Pitti

Giardino di Bóboli

Florence

Santissima
Annunziata

Ospedale
degli
Innocenti

Piazza
G. Salvemini

Santa Croce

400 m

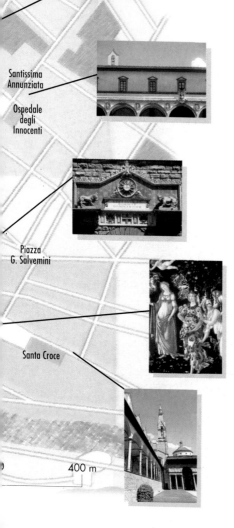

*The many faces
of Florence,
the capital of
Tuscany, symbolize
the spirit of
innovation that
typified the
Renaissance.
Each district
of the city and
each of its
monuments
recalls such
famous names
as Donatello,
Botticelli and
Michelangelo,
Strozzi, Pazzi,
and the Medicis.*

The construction of the imposing Cathedral of Santa Maria del Fiore established Florence as the capital of Tuscany.

Blessed with a glorious past, Tuscany delights visitors with the splendour of its art and variety of its landscapes.

One of Tuscany's many abbeys.

Once upon a time in Tuscany

Visitors who have come in search of the unique charm of this region will be enchanted by the beauty of its landscapes and the elegance of its towns. The gentle way of life that has always been associated with Tuscany was further amplified by the Renaissance movement which began here. At the end of the 16th century, this school of thought overturned medieval principles by placing man at the centre of all knowledge and thus opened up a whole new world to Europe.

With its hilly terrain, Tuscany is often austere in its beauty.

Florence played an important political role in Europe during the Renaissance, having early on acquired the status of banker to its royal courts.

Right: a statue of Cosimo I in Florence. During the 16th century, this Medici ruled Tuscany with a rod of iron.

Bordered by the Apennine chain of mountains and the Mediterranean Sea, Tuscany occupies a central location in Italy. Covering most of the ancient **Etruscan territory**, it can legitimately claim to be the rightful heir to this sophisticated civilization; a claim that it has often used as a pretext to express opposition to its domineering neighbour, Rome. Modern-day Tuscany, however, traces its true roots back to the Middle Ages.

The beautiful Tuscan countryside invites the traveller to stay awhile. The farmhouses built in local stone blend subtly into their natural surroundings.

Given its relative isolation, the Tuscan hinterland is the ideal place for a retreat, as indicated by the many monastic orders that have moved there.

This land of coveted riches is dotted with seemingly invincible citadels.

Siena and the surrounding area retain strong medieval influences in contrast with northern Tuscany which bears the imprint of a particular style of Romanesque art, developed by the artists of Pisa. Later, the Renaissance movement, which came to influence the entire region, helped raise its profile. Florence, a city that was particularly vibrant during this period, soon established itself as the world capital of this 'new culture'.

In the beautiful Tuscan countryside, man seems to have made use of all the elements at hand in the creation of vast magnificent landscapes. Beneath an azure sky, golden fields stretch out over gently rolling hills crowned by dark cypress trees.

In Florence, the Neptune Fountain dominates the Piazza della Signoria. This square has been the backdrop for all kinds of political and popular demonstrations.

The prosperous city of Florence flourished during the Middle Ages before becoming the true capital of Tuscany during the Renaissance.

The Duomo Santa Maria del Fiore.

The Centre of Florence

† Duomo Santa Maria del Fiore

● Museo dell'Opera del Duomo

Battistero

Campanile di Giotto

Piazza della Repubblica

Orsanmichele ●

Via de' Calzaiuoli

Via del Proconsolo

Casa di Dante ●

Via della Condotta

● Bargello

Piazza S. Firenze

Borgo Ss. Apostoli

Loggia della Signoria ● ● Palazzo vecchio

Arno

Ponte Vecchio

● Galleria degli Uffizi

The use of green and white marble confers a unity of style between the Baptistry (foreground, right) and the Duomo, even though the two date from different periods.

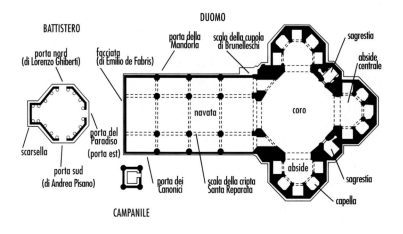

porta della Mandorla — scala della cupola di Brunelleschi — sagrestia

porta nord (di Lorenzo Ghiberti) — facciata (di Emilio de Fabris) — abside centrale

navata — coro

porta del Paradiso (porta est)

scarsella

porta sud (di Andrea Pisano) — porta dei Canonici — scala della cripta Santa Reparata — abside — sagrestia

capella

CAMPANILE

Plan of the Duomo Santa Maria del Fiore, the Baptistry and Giotto's Campanile.

Piazza del Duomo

In the centre of Florence, the immense Cathedral of Santa Maria del Fiore only comes into view as you enter the narrow Piazza del Duomo. Together with the

Following the example set by Pisa, most Tuscan cities used white marble from the hills around the town of Carrara for their religious buildings. Florence, however, rejected this stone in favour of the pink marble of Maremma and the dark green of Prato.

Campanile and the Baptistry, it forms a remarkable architectural ensemble.

The cathedral façade: a symphony in white, green and pink marble.

Many buildings were destroyed to create enough space to build the cathedral. The intended dimensions of the building were, however, enlarged further and the resulting Duomo seems to be rather cramped in its little square. From the surrounding streets, it is often only the dome that can be seen.

In order to outdo the domed cathedrals of Siena and Pisa, Florentines entrusted the architect Arnolfo di Cambio with the building of their Duomo in 1296. At the time of his premature death, however, only the foundations had been completed. His successor, Giotto di Bondone, abandoned work on the cathedral in favour of the **Campanile**. In 1337, Talenti modified the plans, turning them into a massive architectural project.

The Campanile offers this panoramic view of the city. From here, the nave of the Duomo seems completely overwhelmed by the gigantic proportions of the dome.

The Baptistry, Cathedral and Campanile seen from the Piazza San Giovanni.

Above: This detail from the 'Gate of Paradise', sculpted in the 15th century by Lorenzo Ghiberti, represents Moses receiving the Ten Commandments. Right: This church, one of the oldest in Florence, officially became the Baptistry in 1128, at which

point the façade of white and green marble was added. The bronze doors, by Andrea Pisano, date from the 14th century.

In 1380, the construction of the **Duomo**, 509 feet (155 metres) in length, stopped once again because no one knew how to complete a dome with a diameter of 138 feet (42 metres). Forty years later, Filippo Brunelleschi found the solution to this problem and 140 years after it was started, the cathedral was finally consecrated in 1436.

The Campanile stands 279 feet (85 m) tall.

The pyramid-shaped roof of the Baptistry seems rather heavier than the Renaissance dome of the Cathedral. Even so, its lines are as equally elegant.

During the 14th century, the wooden doors of the Roman **Baptistry** were replaced by bronze ones, a material that was deemed to be more noble. Around 1330, the Pisan artist Andrea Pisano sculpted the magnificent South Door and almost a century later, the Florentine authorities commissioned the sculptor Lorenzo Ghiberti to carve the other two.

The Florentines were so impressed by the North Door of the Baptistry, carved by Ghiberti between 1403 and 1424, that they entrusted him with the creation of the third door, facing the cathedral.

To accomplish this masterpiece, which Michelangelo called 'the Gate of Paradise', Ghiberti worked from 1425 to 1452, almost until his death. The goldsmith-sculptor was inspired by scenes from the Old Testament for the panels, which he framed with a frieze of sibyls and prophets.

The choir loft, sculpted by Donatello and Luca della Robbia.

Behind the Cathedral of Santa Maria del Fiore, a large building contains the Museo dell'Opera del Duomo (the **Cathedral Works Museum**). When founded in 1296, the Works were responsible for the building and main-tenance of the Duomo.

Donatello (c. 1386–1466) sculpted this figure of Mary Magdalene when he was 69. The statue captures with astonishing force the anguish suffered by the saint.

When it was opened in 1891, the museum served as a warehouse for the sculptures that originally adorned the Cathedral. The collection, completed by pieces from the

This Pietà by Michelangelo was originally intended to be for his own tomb and represents the artist as Nicodemus supporting Christ. The figure of Mary Magdalene was added later by Daniele da Volterra.

Filippo Brunelleschi

Born in Florence in 1377, Filippo Brunelleschi learnt his crafts as a goldsmith, sculpture, and architect by studying the building techniques used in Ancient Rome. Drawing on this training, he was able to solve the problem of completing the gigantic Duomo of Florence, a task which had begun almost 150 years earlier. Along with the sculptor Donatello and the painter Masaccio, he is one of the founding members of the Tuscan art movement of the Quattrocento (15th century). His work on perspective, faithfully recreated using mathematical formulae, had a significant influence on other artists of the period.

Campanile and the Baptistry, offers an excellent overview of Florentine sculpture from the 13th to the 16th centuries. The ground floor is devoted entirely to the construction of the Duomo, bringing together the statues which were mounted on the façade until 1587. On the mezzanine level stands the Pietà by Michelangelo whilst on the first floor, the choir loft, originally placed above the sacristy doors of the Duomo, is the work of Luca della Robbia and Donatello. The Silversmith's Hall houses the original panels from the 'Gate of Paradise' from the Baptistry.

The patron saints of guilds adorn the façade of the Church of Orsanmichele. These four figures, the patron saints of stonemasons, were carved by Banco.

The house where the poet Dante Alighieri was born in 1265 has since been rebuilt.

The Dante Quarter

The paved streets, vaulted porches and lively atmosphere of the Via del Corso all recall the medieval past of the city. Here in the birth place of Dante Alighieri, the

Dante, the son of an impoverished noble, studied at the universities of both Bologna and Padua. Breaking with tradition, he refused to compose his poems, including his most famous work The Divine Comedy, in Latin, writing them in Italian instead.

visitor is constantly struck by the cultural richness of the district.

After having banished Dante for opposing the establishment that was in favour of the Pope, Florence later honoured his memory by naming a street after him.

In the winding streets, little wine cellars, or fiaschetterie, *serve* crostini *(slices of bread spread with creamed chicken livers and anchovies), washed down with a glass of Chianti Classico.*

In 1337, following the reconstruction of the grain market, responsibility for the decoration of niches was given to the city's guilds. In 1405, as the majority of the niches were still empty, the seigniory imposed a deadline of ten years on the guilds to fulfil their role as artistic patron.

A religious fresco decorated this alley.

Heading south from the Piazza del Duomo, the visitor passes through the medieval quarter of Florence where several imposing fortified houses belonging to 12th- and 13th-century aristocrats have survived. It was in this picturesque district of alleys, covered passages, and stone houses that the poet Dante Alighieri, the famous author of *The Divine Comedy*, lived

24

This fresco, in the Church of Orsanmichele, shows the everyday work of stonemasons.

during the 13th century. The Church of **Orsanmichele** has housed statues of the patron saints of the city's guilds since the 15th century. This church, built in 1337 and originally used as a grain market before it was consecrated for worship in 1347, owes its name to the oratory of San Michele which has long since disappeared.

Above: The sculptor Andrea Orcagna dreamed of creating the most beautiful altar of all time. The result, in Orsanmichele, is this marvel of Gothic inspiration, covered in coloured marble, carved reliefs and cherubs.

Above left: The 14 statues of the patron saints of the city's Arti, or guilds, observe the bustling street life below from their positions in stone niches.

The Gothic architecture of the Bargello houses some superb sculptures.

The National Museum, housed in the Bargello, has a rich collection of sculptures, featuring (right) Mercury by Giambologna, Michelangelo's Bacchus, David by Donatello and Cellini's Mercury. Cellini was born in 1500, and had a varied career: as well as being a goldsmith and an engraver of medals, he was also the author of cloak and dagger novels!

Today, the **Bargello** houses the varied collections of the National Museum. The galleries devoted to the sculptors Cellini, Donatello, Michelangelo, Giambologna and Verrocchio together comprise an essential tour for those who wish to trace the history of Tuscan sculpture from the 14th to the 17th centuries.

A bronze by Giambologna.

At 187 feet (57m), the imposing 12th-century Volognana Tower dominates the façade of the Bargello. When it was built in 1255, this palace was used as the city's town hall.

The museum is also noted for its admirable sculpted ivory pieces and maiolica (Italian Renaissance pottery) which have replaced the appalling instruments of torture that were once used in the Bargello prison. The building itself, built in 1255, was originally the town hall before being turned into the residence of the chief of police and a prison.

Towards the end of the 16th century, the chief of police (or barigel) made the palazzo his home, hence the name 'Bargello'.

This varnished terracotta work by Agostino di Duccio is a reminder that maiolica (pottery making) is a strong tradition in the city. Indeed, it was in Florence that one of the earliest porcelain factories in Europe was established during the 16th century.

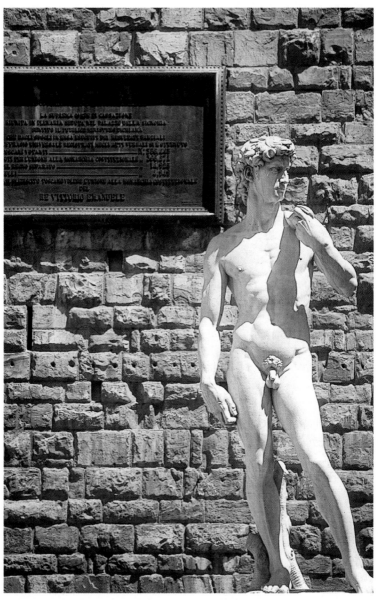

Standing at the entrance of the Palazzo Vecchio, this copy of Michelangelo's David glorifies the courage shown by the Florentines in their fight to establish the Republic.

Neptune *in the Piazza della Signoria is the work of Bartolomeo Ammannati.*

Piazza della Signoria

The Piazza della Signoria has been the setting for Florentine escapades since the Middle Ages. Until the 16th century, the city's political power resided in the Palazzo

Both the Arnolfo Tower and the Palazzo Vecchio have dominated the Piazza della Signoria since the 14th century. Seen here between the buildings of the Ufizzi Gallery, the Arnolfo Tower, on a round pedestal, stands 308 feet (94m) high.

Vecchio where it frequently became embroiled in plots and other schemes.

The entrance to the Palazzo Vecchio is guarded by two Florentine lions.

On the south side of the Piazza della Signoria, adjoining the Palazzo Vecchio, stands the Loggia della Signoria, also known as the Loggia dei Lanzi in memory of the lancers (German mercenaries) who acted as Cosimo I's bodyguards. Once the home of the city's town hall, it now houses a collection of statues, including The Rape of the Sabine Women, *carved by Giambologna in 1583.*

The history of the Piazza della Signoria ('seigniory' or 'city government') goes back to Roman times when it was the site of bathhouses. Subsequently, it became the venue for public festivities, such as executions. The peal of the bells in the tower of the **Palazzo Vecchio**, also known as the Palazzo della Signoria, summoned the

Putto with dolphin *by Verrocchio.*

The narrow door of the Palazzo Vecchio opens onto the Courtyard of Michelozzo, decorated by Vasari for the celebrations of the marriage of Francesco de' Medici and Joanna of Austria in 1565.

Visitors to the Palazzo Vecchio will be able to see the princes' apartments and the rooms in which power was once executed.

citizens to the Piazza where the *Parlamento*, or public meeting, took place. In 1498, the Dominican monk Savonarola was hung and burnt at the stake here after presiding over an austere theocratic republic deemed to be excessively puritanical. Today, the square is home to an impressive collection of statues, including *Perseus* by Cellini (completed in 1554).

Left: Grotesques adorn the ceilings above the grand staircases of the Palazzo Vecchio. This type of whimsical deco- ration was largely inspired by ornamental motifs discovered in the 15th and 16th centuries in the ruins of ancient Italian buildings (known as grottoes).

A detail from Primavera *(1480) in which the painter, Botticelli, revives classical mythology which was very much in vogue during the Renaissance.*

Madonna of the Pomegranate *by Sandro Botticelli.*

In 1560, the Medici family began building the **Uffizi**, between the Palazzo Vecchio and the banks of the Arno, as offices to deal with the administration of the Grand Duchy of Tuscany. Francesco I transformed the second floor of the Uffizi into a gallery in 1581, in which he exhibited the masterpieces accumulated by his family. In 1737, the museum was bequeathed to the city by the last of the Medici's, Maria Lodovica.

During the 16th century, Cosimo I placed the architect Vasari in charge of building the Uffizi. The son of Giovanni delle Bande Neri, Cosimo extended the domination of Florence by conquering the cities of Siena and Luca.

Madonna of the Magnificat *by Sandro Botticelli.*

Constantly enriched by the Medici family, the Uffizi Gallery is the largest art museum in Italy and home to collections from the 13th to the 18th centuries, including The Adoration of the Magi *by Sandro Botticelli and* The Annunciation *by Leonardo da Vinci.*

In the Uffizi Gallery, the presentation of paintings in chronological order traces the advent and development of the Renaissance. With works by Cimabue, Giotto and Martini, the foundation stones of the movement were laid. Ucello, Lippi and Piero della Francesca developed this further, notably by their work on perspective. The golden age of the Renaissance is then marked by Botticelli, Verrocchio and Leonardo da Vinci.

A detail from The Birth of Venus *by Botticelli (c. 1485). The nymph of springtime is shown wrapping Venus in a flowery cloak to conceal her nudity.*

San Lorenzo (right), the Duomo (centre) and the tower of the Palazzo Vecchio (left) seen from the terrace of a cafe on the south bank of the Arno.

The street map of Florence reveals a city organized around its churches which have, in turn, given their names to the various districts.

Sunset over the Arno.

The Districts of Florence

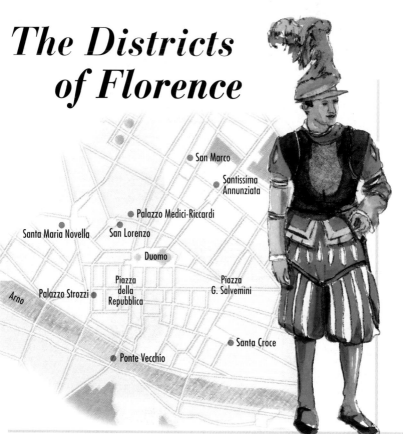

San Marco

Santissima Annunziata

Palazzo Medici-Riccardi

Santa Maria Novella   San Lorenzo

Duomo

Piazza della Repubblica

Arno   Palazzo Strozzi

Piazza G. Salvemini

Santa Croce

Ponte Vecchio

The Santa Croce district fell victim to flooding in 1966 when the waters of the Arno rose to a height of 16 feet (5m) above the walls of the cloisters.

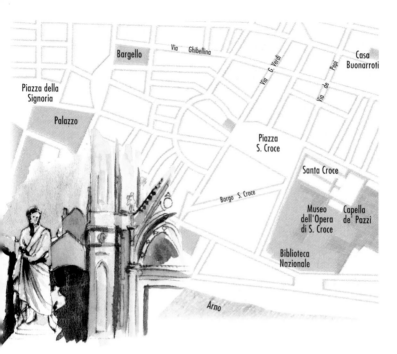

Via Ghibellina

Bargello

Casa Buonarroti

Piazza della Signoria

Via G. Verdi

Via de' Pepi

Palazzo

Piazza S. Croce

Santa Croce

Borgo S. Croce

Museo dell'Opera di S. Croce

Capella de' Pazzi

Biblioteca Nazionale

Arno

The Santa Croce District

During the 14th and 15th centuries, the working-class district of Santa Croce was home to many wool millers. Festivals were a regular part of daily life and today the game of calcio storico is still played annually at the end of June.

This statue of a Franciscan orator recalls a time when mendicant friars attracted large crowds of people in the Piazza Santa Croce to listen to their sermons. The order, founded by St Francis of Assisi, rapidly flourished in Florence.

Brunelleschi drew up the plans for the elegant cloisters of Santa Croce, built in 1455, seven years after his death.

The Piazza Santa Croce is surrounded by typical Florentine palazzos.

In 1228, the Franciscans established their oratory in a little chapel dedicated to the Holy Cross. Rebuilding work on the oratory began in 1294, but was interrupted many times. When it was eventually consecrated by Pope Eugene IV in 1442, the façade was still not finished but **Santa Croce** nevertheless opened its heavy doors to Florentines who wished to attend the services of the religious order founded by St Francis of Assisi.

On every summer solstice (June), the Piazza Santa Croce is transformed into the playing field for 'calcio storico'. Four teams of 27 men, each representing a medieval district of the city, take part using a mixture of fighting and football skills. The prize for the winners is a live cow.

Stained-glass windows dimly light the vast nave of Santa Croce.

The district of Santa Croce attracted the greatest artists and intellectuals of the city. Many of them now lie in the Church of Santa Croce, sometimes referred to as the 'Florentine Pantheon'. The tombs of Michelangelo and Galileo are here, as well as those of other prominent figures. Also on show are monuments honouring the memory of Dante and Machiavelli and epitaphs glorifying Raphael and Leonardo da Vinci.

The remains of Michelangelo, who died in Rome in 1564, were stolen by Florentines and later buried in Santa Croce.

Since 1629, two mannerist fountains by Pietro Tacca have adorned the beautiful Piazza Santissima Annunziata.

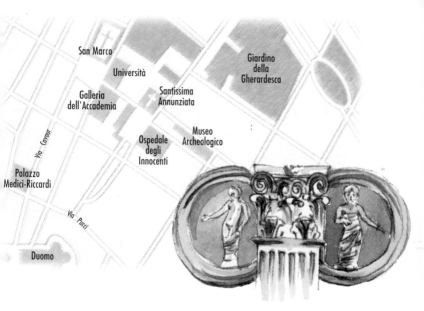

Santissima Annunziata and San Marco

Moving further away from the banks of the fickle Arno, the Florentine people extended their city northwards. In this district, daily life was organized around the

The Church of San Marco, built in the 13th century and since restored many times, is connected to the Convent of San Marco. During the 15th century, Cosimo il Vecchio donated a large sum of money to rebuild the convent and later endowed it with a library.

Church of Santissima Annunziata and the Convent of San Marco.

The 15th-century Spedale degli Innocenti was the first orphanage in Europe.

The entrance to the Church of Santissima Annunziata was modified in the 15th century with donations from the Medici family, enabling Manetti to add an atrium in the Renaissance style, inspired by a drawing by Michelozzo. It was once used to store the wax ex-voto, or boti, offered to the Madonna of the parish, but these were sadly melted down to make candles in 1786.

The Piazza della Santissima Annunziata is lined with elegant buildings which epitomize the delicate spirit of the Renaissance. On one side, the arcades of the **Spedale degli Innocenti** (Foundling Hospital), designed by Brunelleschi, match those of the house of the Order of the Servants of Mary on the other. Opposite the church, the

Santissima Annunziata's baroque ceiling.

A detail from the fresco of the Annunciation on the great baroque dome which covers the choir of Santissima Annunziata.

Each pillar on the façade of the Spedale degli Innocenti is decorated with a medallion of varnished terracotta, the work of Andrea della Robbia.

Palazzo Grifoni is one of only a few Florentine buildings made of brick. The final side is closed by the columns of the Church of **Santissima Annunziata** (the Church of the Holy Annunciation). Its entrance, in the form of an atrium, is decorated with Renaissance frescoes by Andrea del Sarto. Inside, the artist's work is almost lost under baroque ornament.

This little marble shrine, constructed according to Michelozzo's plans, contains a fresco with a reputation for miracles. Shown during major religious festivals, it is said that an angel painted the virgin's face while the painter was asleep.

Michelangelo used a block of marble thought to be unworkable to create the statue of David. Sculpted between 1501 and 1504, David prefigures the baroque style.

The workshop of the School of Sculpture.

The large collection of Florentine paintings on display in the Galleria dell'Accademia often has a religious theme and is of a particularly high quality.

The **Galleria dell'Accademia** (Academy of Fine Art) contains Florentine paintings dating from the 13th century to the Renaissance as well as the unfinished sculptures of the *Quattro Prigioni* (Four Prisoners) by Michelangelo. Intended for the tomb of Pope Julius II, their writhing bodies seem to struggle in an attempt to free themselves from the lifeless marble.

Pierre-Leopold I of Lorraine, who wished to give students at the Academy of Fine Art the opportunity of studying the works of the masters, made several donations to the foundation of the Galleria dell' Accademia.

During the 19th century, the architect Emilio de Fabris designed a gallery filled with light to display Michelangelo's David. Notable amongst the exhibits in the Michelangelo Gallery is the Quattro Prigioni *(Four Prisoners) struggling to escape.*

A 15th-century fresco representing The Annunciation *by Fra Angelico.*

On April 8, 1498, Savonarola, who had taken refuge in the Convent of San Marco, was finally captured.

On the Piazza San Marco, the façade of the convent (1780) is the work of Giaocchino Pronti.

The beautiful architecture and frescoes of the Convent of **San Marco** house almost all the works of one of its most famous occupants, the painter Fra Angelico (c. 1395–1455). Although he took up painting late in life, he was put in charge of decorating the convent by Cosmo il Vecchio in 1436 and it is now a museum dedicated to the memory of the artist. The library (1441) was the first public library in Europe.

Cosimo il Vecchio of the Medici family built the vast library of the Convent of San Marco to enable the public to have access to the collection of Niccolo Nicoli.

Giovanni delle Bande Nere dominates the Piazza di San Lorenzo. His nickname refers to the black banners (bande nere) that he carried after the death of Pope Leon X.

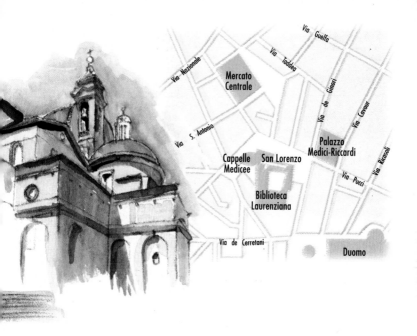

The San Lorenzo District

Home to the Mercato Centrale (central market), San Lorenzo is a hive of Florentine activity. The hustle and bustle pervades every alley, where crowds of chattering customers wander from one shop to another in search of their next purchase.

The coat of arms of the Medici family embellishes the floor of the Chapel of the Princes. Historians believe that the balls, or palle, symbolize coins, pills or the weights of money-changers. The origins of this family of doctors or apothecaries who became prosperous merchants and bankers are not without mystery!

A detail from one of the two pulpits in San Lorenzo, sculpted by Donatello. It is from here that Savonarola delivered his most denunciatory sermons.

In the foundations of the New Sacristy, an underground gallery is decorated with drawings attributed to the artist and sculptor Michelangelo.

The dome of the Chapel of the Princes.

The Medici coat of arms decorates the entrance to the Church of San Lorenzo which was commissioned in 1423 by Giovanni de' Medici, known as Giovanni di Bicci. The architect, Brunelleschi, created an amazingly light building through skilful use of the colours of different building materials.

It was in the San Lorenzo district, where they began their rise to power, that the Medici family commissioned works from the great artists of their time. The Church of **San Lorenzo** owes its splendour to the collaboration between the architect Brunelleschi and the sculptor Donatello, who transformed the church during the 15th century. The Old Sacristy is a perfect example of how the

Magnificent sculptures by Michelangelo adorn the tombs of the Medici family.

two complemented each other artistically. By 1516, the façade of the church had still not been added and designs were commissioned from Michelangelo. Unfortunately, his plans were deemed too expensive and even today, the front wall remains bare. The great master more than compensated for this by creating sculptures for the Medici family mausoleum.

A visit to the cloister gardens gives visitors the opportunity to appreciate the monumental staircase to the Laurentian Library, designed by Michelangelo. The Chapel of the Princes houses the remains of six grand dukes of Tuscany who lie in marble tombs. The New Sacristy and the Chapel of the Princes constitute the mausoleum of the Medici family.

The huge Palazzo Medici-Riccardi contains some precious treasures.

The chapel of the Palazzo Medici-Riccardi is beautifully decorated with magnificent frescoes which include The Procession of the Magi, *painted by Benozzo Gozzoli (15th century). The* cortile, *or inner courtyard, forms a sumptuous setting for* Bandinelli's Orpheus *(right).*

Overlooking the Piazza San Lorenzo and behind an austere façade, the **Palazzo Medici-Riccardi** hides a courtyard framed by a colonnade, a veritable masterpiece of elegance and proportion. During the 15th century, Cosimo de' Medici, known as 'il Vecchio' (the Elder), completely changed the area when building his palazzo, demolishing several houses and widening the present-day Via Cavour. Brunelleschi was

Baroque frescoes decorate the ceilings of the Palazzo Medici-Riccardi.

commissioned to draw up the original plans but these were considered too lavish, and the work was finally entrusted to Michelozzo di Bartolomeo. Built in 1444, the palazzo was sold to the Riccardi family in 1655, after the Medicis took up residence in the Palazzo Pitti. The new inhabitants enlarged the building, to the detriment of the garden. Despite the austerity of its exterior, this square building became the model for all the grandiose Florentine residences of the Renaissance. At the centre of the house, the gracious courtyard and its topiary garden was once used as the setting for lavish receptions.

A walk among the statues in the delightful gardens of Palazzo Medici-Riccardi is the ideal end to any visit. The statue of David by Donatello, which once stood here, is now in the Bargello.

The façade of the Church of Santa Maria Novella, inlaid with polychrome marble, stands on a Gothic base and is mounted by a Renaissance portal.

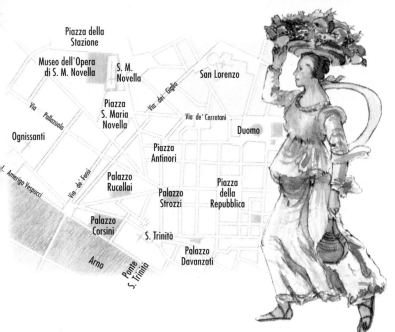

Piazza della Stazione

Museo dell'Opera di S. M. Novella

S. M. Novella

San Lorenzo

Via dei Giglio

Via Pallazuolo

Piazza S. Maria Novella

Via de' Cerretani

Duomo

Ognissanti

Via de' Fossi

Piazza Antinori

S. Amerigo Vespucci

Palazzo Rucellai

Palazzo Strozzi

Piazza della Repubblica

Palazzo Corsini

S. Trinità

Arno

Ponte S. Trinità

Palazzo Davanzati

Santa Maria Novella and the Piazza della Repubblica

The area of Santa Maria Novella has not lost any of its social prestige and is still the epitome of Florentine luxury. The ornate façade of the church and the size of the surrounding palazzos bear witness to the former wealth of Florence.

No one should visit the Piazza della Repubblica without sampling the refreshments at one of its many cafes (the famous Gilli is pictured here). Apart from the traditional Italian espresso, you can choose from a wide variety of ice creams and pastries.

Roman influences are apparent in the triangular pediment of Santa Maria Novella.

The Church of Santa Maria Novella bears witness to many different architectural styles yet the façade is in no way marred by its many sources of inspiration. Indeed, the whole is unified by two elegant volutes.

The greatest concentration of palazzos in Florence is found in the area of Santa Maria Novella. Rich merchants and bankers demolished houses to build their residences here and each of these powerful families owned a chapel in one of the numerous churches in the area. During the 15th century, one wealthy merchant, Giovanni Rucellai, even paid for the completion of the façade of the Church of **Santa Maria Novella**. The polychrome marble façade was built by Dominicans during the 13th and 14th centuries and subsequent Gothic and Renaissance modifications have not

The interior of Santa Maria Novella contains a superb fresco by Ghirlandaio.

detracted from its simplicity or harmony. The elegance of the interior decoration is evidence of the fortunes accumulated by the great families of the area. The Gondi Chapel, for example, still houses Brunelleschi's magnificent crucifix, which rivals that of the Strozzi Chapel, attributed to Giotto. All of the chapels are decorated with frescoes, the most remarkable of which were painted by Ghirlandaio.

The Trinity by Masaccio, painted on the left-hand side of the aisle of the Church of Santa Maria Novella in 1427, was the first fresco to incorporate the mathematical rules of perspective, as defined by Brunelleschi. The great beauty of this work has inspired many painters.

Smart shops have now opened near the Santa Trinita Bridge.

On the route back to the historic centre of the city stand the prestigious residences of prosperous drapers and bankers. The size and elegance of the **Palazzo Strozzi** reflects the ambitions of the Strozzi family, who once challenged the power of

The Florentine passion for the finer things in life is epitomized by the traditional fiaschetterie, those little wine cellars serving crostini snacks.

the Medicis. During the 15th century, Filippo Strozzi, a rich banker, bought and demolished over a dozen properties and replaced them with his huge three-storey palazzo.

An essential part of the Florentine way of life is the the scooter. It is able to weave in and out of the congested narrow streets of the city centre and can be easily parked between two cars.

Florence, the capital of fashion

Between the Santa Trinita Bridge and the Piazza della Repubblica, the fashion houses of famous Italian designers are the worthy successors to the prosperous drapers that were once found there during the Renaissance period. In beautiful buildings, up-to-the-minute boutiques dictate future fashions. Even the Palazzo Strozzi, a symbolic monument of this wealthy area of Florence, occasionally gets caught up in the world of designers when it hosts fashion shows.

A Roman forum once stood on the site of . the **Piazza della Repubblica**, which itself replaced the Mercato Vecchio (Old Market). The Piazza, stripped of its medieval charm during alterations at the end of the 19th century, is now *the* place to meet. The in-crowd flocks to the open-air cafes around the square where elegant young women can be seen rubbing shoulders with preoccupied businessmen. Whilst the square was once the venue for literary debates at the beginning of the century, it is now the shop window for the world of high fashion.

Florence has long since turned its back on the Arno, preferring to develop away from the unpredictable banks of the river.

Oltrarno, the historic area on the south bank of the Arno, delights visitors with its palazzos, gardens, and rustic charm.

The terraces of the Boboli Gardens.

Oltrarno

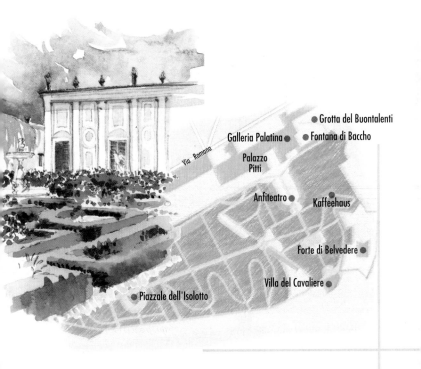

Grotta del Buontalenti

Galleria Palatina

Fontana di Baccho

Via Romana

Palazzo Pitti

Anfiteatro

Kaffeehaus

Forte di Belvedere

Villa del Cavaliere

Piazzale dell'Isolotto

Despite the violent flood waters of the river and the bombs of World War II, the Ponte Vecchio has survived, much to the pleasure of visitors and shopkeepers alike.

The three arches of the Ponte Vecchio straddle the Arno at its narrowest point.

To reach **Oltrarno** on the south bank of the Arno, pedestrians must cross the city's oldest bridge, the Ponte Vecchio. As visitors walk across the bridge, they will inevitably be tempted to visit the many shops built on it. By the 16th century, it was so congested that the Medicis built a private passage above the craftsmen's workshops and stalls. They could then reach the south bank without having to mingle with the crowds.

Vasari built the private corridor crossing the Ponte Vecchio in just six months. The section that adjoins the Uffizi Gallery houses magnificent works by the likes of David, Titian and Rubens. The corridor, however, is not open to the public and can only be admired from the outside.

The setting sun casts an ochre light over the Ponte Vecchio.

Allow half a day for a visit to the Palazzo Pitti and about an hour for a walk around the magnificent Boboli Gardens.

The façade of the Palazzo Pitti extends along the whole length of the Piazza Pitti.

After the original bridge was destroyed by flood waters in 1333, construction of the present **Ponte Vecchio** began in 1345. As a link between two commercial districts, it was very soon overtaken by tanners and fishmongers who regularly threw their waste into the river. This irritated those in power to such an extent that these professions were banished from the bridge at the end of the 16th century, to be replaced by goldsmiths.

Two wings, built in the 18th century, frame the entrance to the Palazzo Pitti.

The Medici family regularly crossed the Arno, from the Palazzo Vecchio, the centre of political power, to the **Palazzo Pitti** (Pitti Palace). The history of this palazzo once again illustrates the rivalries that existed between opposing wealthy Florentines. The banker Luca Pitti commissioned the first stage of this building in 1458 to show that he could outdo the Medicis. The cost of building the palace unfortunately bankrupted the Pitti family and in 1540, Cosimo I bought the unfinished palazzo for the Medicis and enlarged it still further.

The Medicis invited the 17th-century masters of baroque art, notably Pietro da Corna, to decorate their private apartments. As a result, these sumptuous residences are packed with magnificent works of art.

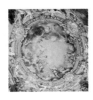

King Vittorio Emanuele II of Savoy ruled Italy from this throne from 1860 to 1870.

Political power crossed the Arno when the Medicis moved home to the Palazzo Pitti. It was there that they received all of the city's influential figures, such as ambassadors, businessmen, and, of course, many courtesans, who all admired the splendour of the palazzo and its gardens.

In 1560, Cosimo I left the Palazzo Vecchio to move to the Palazzo Pitti. After the alterations by the architect Parigi, which began in 1620, the façade of the palazzo tripled in length, exceeding 650 feet (200 metres). It was later home to the Italian royal family before becoming state property. Today, the State Apartments are open to the public, as is the prestigious **Palatine Gallery** with its superb collection of Italian paintings.

The collection of Italian paintings from the 16th to the 18th century, acquired by several generations of the Medici family, is displayed in the Palatine Gallery.

Stone tiers add to the Roman character of the open air amphitheatre.

Boboli Hill, named after a former owner, stretches out behind the Palazzo Pitti. On the slopes of this hill, the Medicis created one of the finest 'Italianate' gardens of the Renaissance period. The sculptor Niccolo Pericoli, a pupil of Michelangelo,

Above: La Grotta Grande sculpted by Buontalenti. Left: The Bacchus Fountain, leaning against the walls of the Palazzo Pitti, represents Cosimo I's court dwarf.

was inspired by the landscape to create a stylized version of nature in keeping with the conventions of his period. Dotted with fountains and statues, the gardens lend

The Neptune Fountain, built by Lorenzi between 1565 and1568, is one of the many fountains in the Boboli Gardens. The baroque statue of the god of the sea stands in the middle of a large basin.

themselves to romantic reverie. The open-air amphitheatre, set in a natural hollow, recalls the splendour of the festivities that once took place there. During the Renaissance, this landscape was embellished with hedges clipped into geometrical forms and animal shapes, in accordance with the aesthetic revival of the period. Halfway up the hill, a stop at the Kaffeehaus enables visitors to quench their thirst in an 18th-century rococo setting. Near the top, the Knight's Pavilion houses a large collection of porcelain tableware and the summit itself offers a magnificent view over Florence.

The Expulsion of Adam and Eve

A detour to the Church of Santa Maria del Carmine, situated in the western part of Oltrarno, provides a fitting conclusion to any visit to Florence. The main attraction of the church is found on the walls of the Brancacci Chapel. In 1424, Felice Brancacci commissioned Masolino da Panicale to paint a series of frescoes depicting the life of St Peter. The master worked on them with his pupil, Masaccio, who created scenes of incredibly powerful expression. A notable example is the fresco showing Adam and Eve being driven out of the Garden of Eden. The talented pupil devoted his attention to applying the rules of mathematical perspective, as defined by Brunelleschi.

In northern Tuscany, and especially Pisa, Roman architecture was heavily influenced by the Lombard style and oriental aesthetics.

I n the north of Tuscany, between the foothills of the Apennines and the Ligurian Sea, there lie two proud cities: Pisa and Lucca.

A landscape in northern Tuscany.

Northern Tuscany

*In the Campo dei Miracoli, the Duomo, Baptistry, Campanile and Campo Santo
form an impressive architectural ensemble.*

Camposanto
Campanile
Duomo
Museo
dell'Opera
del Duomo
Battistero
Museo
delle Sinopie
Via Santa Maria
Palazzo
dei Cavalieri
Orto
Botanico
S. Stefano
Via Roma
Palazzo
Agostini
Palazzo
Upezzinghi
Via Risorgimento
Arno
S. Nicola
S. Maria
della Spina
Corso Italia
S. Martino
L. Sonnino Sidney
Via F. Crispi
Citadella
Via Giordano Bruno
Piazza
Vittorio
Emanuele II

Pisa

Pisa was founded and developed on an area of marshland on the Ligurian coast. As a sea port, Pisa soon enjoyed a formidable rise in prominence, power and wealth.

The beautifully intricate mosaics of the Duomo are heavily inspired by Byzantine art and set off by the brilliant white marble used in its construction. The façade, with its numerous galleries and columns, is a model of Romano-Pisan art.

Today, its world-famous leaning tower stands as a reminder of this period.

The Baptistry of Pisa basks in a deeply mystical atmosphere. The superb pulpit sculpted by Nicola Pisano stands opposite the baptismal fonts.

The mathematician, physicist and astronomer Galileo (1564–1642), studied and taught at the University of Pisa. Apart from studying the orbit of the Earth around the Sun, he also carried out experiments on falling objects by dropping them from the top of the Campanile.

A masterpiece of Romano-Pisan architecture, the Duomo was built with the spoils from the capture of Palermo. Around the top section, the series of columns give the façade an impression of lightness. The top itself is crowned with a statue by Andrea Pisano.

The white marble Baptistry of Pisa.

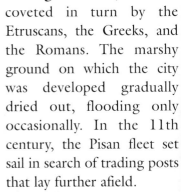

Strategically positioned near the mouth of the Arno on the **Ligurian Sea**, Pisa was coveted in turn by the Etruscans, the Greeks, and the Romans. The marshy ground on which the city was developed gradually dried out, flooding only occasionally. In the 11th century, the Pisan fleet set sail in search of trading posts that lay further afield.

This coat of arms of the Knights of the Crusades is found in the Campo Santo cemetery. At the beginning of the 13th century, soil was brought here from the Holy Land.

The mosaics decorating the Duomo of Pisa are Byzantine in influence.

The Pisans pursued the Moors around the Mediterranean, seizing fabulous booty along the way, and later subjugated Corsica, Sardinia, and the Balearic Islands. Pisa became rich thanks to its maritime empire and began building splendid monuments. In the **Campo Dei Miracoli** ('Field of Miracles'), the Pisans erected a Romanesque Duomo, combining classical influences with colours of the Orient.

The southern gallery of the Campo Santo is decorated with 15th-century frescoes by Gozzoli illustrating scenes from the Old Testament.

At the far corners of its second colonnade, the Duomo of Pisa is adorned with the statues of two evangelists, that were created in the workshop of Pisano (late 13th century).

The Leaning Tower

Work on the Campanile began in 1173 but was stopped when the marshy ground began to subside inspite of drainage. Construction work was suspended for 90 years and finally completed in 1350 when Tommaso Pisano crowned the leaning tower with a bell chamber, raising it to a height of 180 feet (55 m). During the 16th century, Pisari, concerned that the Campanile might collapse, managed to stabilize the base by shoring it up. However, the spongy soil of the region did not offer sufficient resistance and the tower started moving again. During the 19th century, attempts to drain the land produced a catastrophic effect, further weakening the ground.

Although its construction lasted from 1063 until the beginning of the 13th century, it displays a remarkable coherence of style. The **Baptistry** (1152–1284), also begun in Romanesque style, tends towards Gothic ornateness on its second storey. Work on the final building, the **Campanile**, began towards the end of the 12th century continuing the motif of arcatures mounted on colonnaded galleries already used in the Duomo and Baptistry. After the completion of the third storey, however, the ground began to subside, giving the tower its famous incline.

Having drained its marshy ground, Pisa then had to tame the Arno.

Two aquatic festivals celebrate Pisa's glorious past: the Regatta di Ranieri (17 June), and the Gioco del Ponte (the last Sunday in June).

Visitors attracted by the famous Leaning Tower should not overlook charming medieval alleys.

During the 13th century, Pisa, having taken advantage of the crusades to extend its influence throughout the Mediterranean, was in permanent competition with the rapidly expanding port of Genoa. This competition led, inevitably, to conflict. In 1284, the two fleets clashed at the Battle of Meloria, at which the Pisans were forced to submit to the Genoans. As a result, the influence of Pisa suffered an inevitable decline.

In the old part of Pisa, many façades are decorated with unusual frescoes.

During the course of the 15th century, Pisa gradually lost all of its trading posts in the Mediterranean. Taking advantage of this situation, the Florentines captured the city in 1406 after a long and arduous siege. As a result, Pisa was demoted to a mere provincial capital. This Tuscan city, which was the first to profit from turning its attentions to the rest of the world, was condemned to play a minor role from then on. To discover the true Pisan way of life, leave the Campo dei Miracoli to those tourists who are in a hurry and explore the many narrow paved streets of the old districts.

A walk around the centre of Pisa gives visitors the opportunity to see the delightful coloured façades and fortified housed of the 12th century. They can also visit the market which is held on the left bank of the Arno.

This Virgin and Child adorns the right corner of the façade of the Church of San Michele in Foro, the finest example of Romano-Pisan architecture in Lucca.

A quiet forest retreat in the mountains of Vetricia.

Lucca and the Apuan Alps

Perched on a spur of land, the medieval city of Lucca is the gateway to the Apuan Alps. To the north, the steep slopes make commercial forestry difficult but the

Even in this remote area, the Tuscan love of art is still evident. At the 17th-century Villa Mansi just outside Lucca, for example, there is an art gallery devoted to 18th-century Renaissance paintings.

region has been able to profit from thermal spas and deposits of marble.

The Allegorical Dream Chamber *ends the tour of the apartments of the Villa Mansi.*

The town of Lucca was the birth place of P u c c i n i , Catalani, and Geminiani, and annually hosts music festivals.

The sumptuous apartments of the Villa Mansi proudly display their opulent baroque and rococo styles.

Not far from Pisa, the town of **Lucca** is surrounded by thick red brick walls. Its history dates back to 180 BC when it was little more than a Roman colony. Roman influences are still apparent in the city centre where the streets are perfectly straight. In the Middle Ages, Lucca became rich and famous thanks to silk, which it produced and exported to markets throughout the world. Having been under the rule of Pisa

Lucca retained its independence until the end of the 18th century.

and Florence for a time, Lucca enjoyed a long period of peace and prosperity following its independence in 1369. It was only some 430 years later that Napoleon's Italian campaign disrupted this harmony. Renaissance art made little impression on Luccan architecture and San Paolino remains the only church to be embellished by this movement. The rest of the city bears witness to the Romano-Pisan style, as seen in the Church of San Michele in Foro. Even the intricate inlaid façade of the medieval Duomo, dedicated to St Martin, is Romano-Pisan in style.

In the Duomo at Lucca, a wooden 13th-century crucifix is linked to the legend of Volto Santo. It is claimed that this crucifix, on which Christ's head is said to have been sculpted by an angel and his body by Nicodemus, crossed the sea from Palestine in a drifting boat. On its arrival in Italy, a cart drawn by wild oxen and driven by God's will is said to have carried the cross to Lucca.

Numerous isolated villages cling to the mountain sides.

In the Vetricia Mountains, water has played an important part in creating the beauty of the landscape.

For over two thousand years, the quality of the marble from the Apuan Alps has been highly prized, first by the Romans and later by Leonardo da Vinci and Michelangelo who went in person to Carrara to choose their stone.

Heading up the Lugurian coast towards Pisa, the Versilia coastal strip becomes progressively narrower. On the outskirts of Massa, the Apennine chain suddenly rises to over 6500 feet (2000 metres) at its highest point. Since Roman times, the excellent **Carrara** marble has been quarried from this mountain range.

The thermal spa of Montecatini.

At Borgo a Mozzano, the daring architect of the Ponte del Diavolo (Devil's Bridge) took his inspiration from an extraordinary legend from the 12th century.

Once the bridge was built, it was rumoured that the architect had made a pact with the devil in order to stop it from collapsing.

Further to the east, the Serchio River flows towards Lucca between the Apennine mountains and those of the Apuan Alps. Beyond this narrow fertile valley, the mountainous **Garfagnana** region has few natural resources. Numerous hamlets, almost unchanged since the Middle Ages, preserve Roman churches and a rich store of folk legends.

At Pinocchio Park in Collodi, adults and children are able to relive the adventures of the wooden puppet who came to life. The mother of Carlo Lorenzini, the author, used to live in this little village where the theme park has been built.

The ravages of time have served only to deepen the mystical atmosphere that pervades the Cistercian ruins of the Abbey of San Galgano in the woodlands outside Siena.

To the east of Florence, the only signs of life are those of isolated monasteries and the fortified cities of Arezzo and Cortona.

Cypress trees flank the winding roads.

The Tuscan
Hinterland

Camaldoli

Firenze   Vallombrosa
          Poppi   *Casentino*   La Verna

Arno

Arezzo

Eremio San Egidio
Siena
                Cortona
Elsa
        Crete
        Monte Oliveto Maggiore
San Galgano

At the end of the 9th century, the Benedictine monk Guido Monaco invented the system of musical notation that enabled music to be preserved in writing.

Michelangelo was born in the little village of Caprese in 1475.

Arezzo and the Casentino

The Casentino, a vast territory surrounded by high mountains, developed away from the fray of western Tuscany, attracting many religious orders that found peace and tranquillity in the wooded hills to the north of the city of Arezzo.

While the region of the Casentino was spared by the Medicis, Arezzo could not escape their clutches. The pure determination radiating from the statue of Cosimo I (left) conveys the character of a man who would rather depopulate a city than lose it.

The charming buildings of the Piazza Grande in Arezzo.

The origins of Arezzo date back to the Etruscan era (8th–4th centuries BC). Located in the foothills of the Apennines, dominating the Arno valley, the city's strategic position made it the target of Roman interest. Having initially fought off

Situated at the opening of the Casentino valley, Arezzo, one of the richest cities in Tuscany, has all the charm of a provincial town.

Roman advances, **Arezzo** eventually sided with its conquerors and the city retains many monuments from the prosperous era that followed. In the 13th century, Arezzo

The shadow of the Medicis still hovers on the façades of the buildings in Arezzo. These streets have also been graced by the figures of the poet Petrarch (1304–1374) and the painter and biographer Giorgio Vasari (1511–1574), both natives of Arezzo.

The Chimera of Arezzo

In ancient times, Arezzo, together with eleven other cities, formed the country of Eturia. Arezzo retains many traces of this glorious past, including an astounding piece of sculpture that was excavated during the 16th century. This bronze statue, from the 4th century BC, is of a mythological monster known as a chimera, and is almost certainly of Etruscan origin. The mythological animal is a lion with a goat's head on its back and a serpent's head at the end of its tail. The chimera, which belonged to the collection of Cosimo I, is now on display at the Archeological Museum of Florence.

entered the fratricidal conflict which divided the Tuscan cities and was eventually subjugated by Florence in 1384. The city never recovered from this conflict and suffered a continuous decline, largely due to the indifference of the Medici family. Arezzo, compared by some to Florence because of its beautiful architecture, nevertheless boasts several masterpieces. Simply push open the heavy doors to the Gothic Church of San Francesco and admire the magnificent frescoes of the *The Legend of the True Cross*, painted by Piero della Francesca between 1452 and 1466.

The Castello di Poppi towers proudly above Poppi and the Casentino.

Nature lovers should put on their walking boots to discover the treasures of the Casentino region. The lucky ones may spot a chamois or ibex in the valleys between isolated villages.

The **Casentino**, a vast basin stretching the length of the Apennines, has always served as a refuge during times of flooding in Tuscany. In this remote area, the only traces of life are the fortified castles and isolated abbeys. Inside the Castello di Poppi, a powerful citadel from the 13th and 14th centuries, the counts of Guidi dominated the region at a time when the fortified city of Poppi was the capital of the Casentino.

At Camaldoli, the order of hermits founded by St Rumbold follows Benedictine rule.

At the dawn of the 11th century, St Giovanni Gualberto Visdomini, on a spiritual retreat, founded the monastery of Vallombrosa in the depths of the forest. The reclusive order of San Romualdo (St Rumbold) decided to settle near the village of **Camaldoli** in 1012 where, until the beginning of the 20th century, the hospice cared for the sick free of charge. The surrounding woodland has been a National Park since 1991. It was in the Casentino that the poet Dante Alighieri found refuge when forced to flee Florence at the beginning of the 14th century.

The monks at the minuscule hermitage of Camaldoli conduct tours of the 18th-century church, which reveals a startlingly sumptuous decor in the Neapolitan baroque style.

A statue of St Francis of Assisi in the Monastery of La Verna.

The Monastery of La Verna is a major pilgrimage centre where visitors can stay for a maximum of three days.

St Francis of Assisi founded the Monastery of La Verna on the slopes of Monte Verna in 1213. Visions of the Virgin and Christ, as well as the stigmata that marked St Francis in 1224, have made it a popular place of pilgrimage.

Close to the border with Umbria, many pilgrims make their way to Monte Verna to visit the Monastery of **La Verna**, founded by St Francis of Assisi at the beginning of the 13th century. Count Orlando Cattani, fascinated by the devotion of the monks to the poor, gave the entire mountain to the order of St Francis. The Chapel of the

An enchanting forest on the Monte Verna.

Famous for its works by the Florentine artist della Robbia (1435-1525), the Monastery of La Verna also boasts a number of equally impressive architectural features.

A visit to the Monastery of La Verna and the Museum of the Sanctuary may be followed by a climb on Mount Penna.

Stigmata was built on the site where St Francis saw a vision of the Virgin and Christ in 1224, during which he was marked with the stigmata. The saint was known as *il Poverello* ('the poor man') by his friars since he slept on the ground in a cave in accordance with his vow of poverty. Those in search of solitude will enjoy a walk in the surrounding forest.

The churches of the Monastery of La Verna are decorated with splendid ceramic reliefs by della Robbia. The most famous of these are: The Annunciation, The Adoration of the Child, The Ascension *and* The Crucifixion.

If you take the time to explore the porches and courtyards of Cortona, you will find many statues and sculptures to admire.

The Abbey of San Galgano retains traces of Cistercian influences.

Cortona and the Abbeys of Central Tuscany

Standing at the intersection of the routes linking Siena and Florence with Umbria, Cortona has rarely been able to enjoy the peace and quiet of the Crete, an

Only small villages were established in the desolate region known as the Crete. The houses built on its clay soil are more modest than in the rest of Tuscany but, even so, their owners take care to decorate them to blend in with their surroundings.

area to the east where several religious orders chose to establish themselves.

The Museo Diocesano of Cortona is in the former Church of Gesù (15th–16th centuries).

The rich collection of paintings in the Museo Diocesano includes the superb reredos of the Annunciation, painted by Fra Angelico.

The dome of Santa Maria Nuova, Cortona.

Right: A typical Tuscan scene: blue skies, ochre light, a wrought-iron gate, a vine clinging to the walls...all of which evoke a peaceful way of life and the beauty of the region's landscape. This enchanting picture emerges as the evening sun bathes the scene in golden light.

South of Arezzo, the medieval city of **Cortona** guards the entrance to the fertile Chiana Valley from the rocky spur on which it stands. Built on Etruscan fortifications, Cortona still retains its thick medieval city walls. A veritable lookout post, the city attracted many invaders before finally submitting to Naples in 1409. The latter then sold it

The imposing citadel of Cortona has guarded the city since the Middle Ages.

The quiet rustic charm of Cortona is conducive to spending a relaxing holiday.

to Florence a couple of years later. Inside the city walls, visitors will find a marvellous collection of medieval houses and Renaissance buildings. The Duomo, built on the remains of a Roman church, was designed by Giuliano da Sangallo in the 16th century. The portal and campanile complete this graciously proportioned ensemble.

Completed during the 19th century in a neo-Gothic style, the rose window of the Church of Santa Margherita is set in the 17th-century bell tower. The original sanctuary was built during the 14th century to house the remains of St Margherita of Cortona.

The cells of the Franciscan friars of the Eremo (hermitage) of San Egidio della Celle.

In the olive groves at the bottom of the foothills of Cortona, the Church of Santa Maria delle Grazie testifies to the lightness and linear purity of the Renaissance. Its Sienese architect Francesco di Giorgio Martini was inspired by the work of Brunelleschi.

In Cortona, as in Arezzo, religious buildings display a quality of humility rare in Tuscany due to the presence of a great number of monasteries in the vicinity of these isolated towns. At the foot of Cortona's walls, the rather unassuming façade of the Church of **Santa Maria delle Grazie** conceals a beautifully proportioned interior with a number of 16th-century stained-glass windows by Guillaume de Marcillat.

St Francis of Assisi established his first community at San Egidio della Celle, near Cortona, on his return from Rome where the Pope had officially recognized the order.

The Olivetans, a Benedictine order, settled in the Crete.

In summer, fields of wheat cover the sides of the hill on which the Monastery of Monte Oliveto Maggiore stands.

At Monte Oliveto Maggiore, tourists are able to visit the refectory, the Great Cloister

(1427–1474), and the library containing 14th-and 15th-century manuscripts. There are also tours of the pharmacy and the church.

In contrast to the reclusive orders who took to the impenetrable forests of the foothills of the Apennines, the Benedictines founded the Abbey of **Monte Oliveto Maggiore** on the edge of the Crete region. On the hilltop, cloaked by cypress trees, the Olivetan monastery overlooks the farmlands dotted around the valley below.

The tilled clay soil of the Crete.

Behind the fortified gates, a path flanked by cypress trees leads to the buildings that make up the 15th-century Abbey of Monte Oliveto Maggiore.

At the top of the hill, the pink bricks of the Abbey of Monte Oliveto Maggiore are concealed by a screen of cypress trees.

In the barren area of the **Crete**, the rare sight of trees inevitably indicates the existence of a hamlet. Stretching from Cortona to Siena, the hills of pallid clay form a desolate landscape at the heart of the fertile region of Tuscany. The grey and white clay soil does not lend itself easily to the cultivation of crops and creates a somewhat lunar landscape.

At Monte Oliveto Maggiore, the 15th-century cloisters are beautifully decorated with frescoes depicting the life of St Benedict. The first nine were painted by Signorelli and the remaining 27 were completed by Sodoma in 1508.

The Cistercian monks settled on the spot where St Galgano built his hut.

Inside the chapel of San Galgano Montesiepi stands a sword embedded in a lump of stone. According to legend, when the knight Galgano tried to break his sword on a rock in renunciation of war, the stone swallowed the blade. The knight saw this as a sign from God and became a hermit.

South of Siena, amidst the hills of the Crete, the ruins of the Abbey of **San Galgano** exude an atmosphere of profound religious devotion. Only the walls of the church and chapter house survive today, as a reminder of the most important Cistercian Gothic building erected in Italy during the 13th century. These remaining sections of wall may remind visitors of another building: they served as a model for the Duomo at Siena.

The Cisterian Gothic Abbey of San Galgano was allowed to fall into decline at the end of the 14th century.

Around the delightful Piazza del Campo, the medieval heart of Siena displays every nuance of colour from ochre to dark brown.

At the centre of Tuscany, San Gimignano and Siena have survived almost intact since the Middle Ages behind their fortified walls.

Fortified houses in San Gimignano.

Central Tuscany

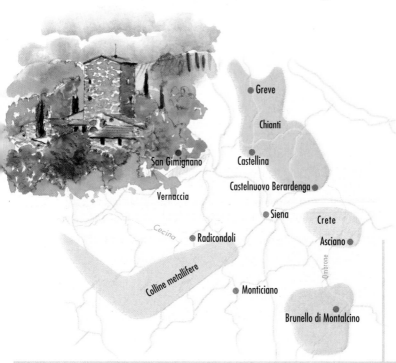

Greve

Chianti

San Gimignano

Castellina

Castelnuovo Berardenga

Vernaccia

Cecina

Siena

Crete

Radicondoli

Asciano

Ombrone

Colline metallifere

Monticiano

Brunello di Montalcino

The Torre del Mangia overlooks the medieval town below, with its tightly packed houses, fortified towers and narrow winding streets.

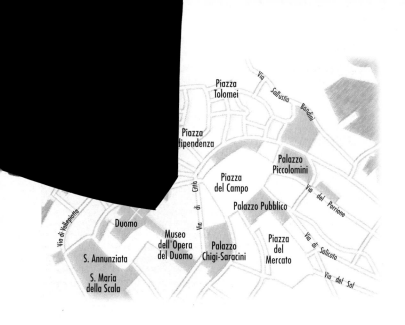

Piazza Tolomei

Via Sallustio

Bandini

Piazza Indipendenza

Palazzo Piccolomini

Piazza del Campo

Via del Porrione

Via di Città

Palazzo Pubblico

Via di Vallepiatta

Duomo

Museo dell'Opera del Duomo

Palazzo Chigi-Saracini

Piazza del Mercato

Via di Salicoto

S. Annunziata

Piazza del Mercato

Via del Sol

S. Maria della Scala

Siena

Siena's narrow streets and palazzos, almost all ochre in colour, are built on three adjacent hills. The sumptuous buildings testify to the city's commercial wealth which aroused the jealousy of its constant historical rival, Florence.

On the highest point in Siena, the Cathedral of Santa Maria Assunta is decorated with alternating bands of black and white marble. The Romanesque style of the colonnaded openings on the campanile has obvious Pisan influences.

The medieval city centre is inaccessible to large vehicles. Small Italian cars are ideal for getting to the Duomo.

The three triangular pediments of the Cathedral of Santa Maria Assunta are decorated with 19th-century mosaics.

A chapel in Santa Maria Assunta.

Inside the Duomo of Siena, a subtle play of light illuminates the ornamental pavement that consists of 37 panels of marble marquetry and was created between 1359 and 1547. The composition depicts important events in the Christian religion.

From the 12th century onwards, **Siena** sent its merchants and bankers to work in all of Europe's markets and courts. Confident of its power, Siena defied papal authority by rejecting its bishop in 1167 and sided with the Ghibellines. Towards the end of the Middle Ages, Siena's prosperity gradually declined as a result of its constant conflict with the Guelph

The Campanile and Duomo seen from the roof of the Museo dell'Opera del Duomo.

faction, led by Florence, but continued to grow in size, adorning itself with palazzos and churches. Many of these illustrate the development of the Gothic style preceding the Renaissance. At the beginning of the 13th century, Duccio di Buoninsegna founded the Sienese school of painting, drawing inspiration from Byzantine compositions.

The Museo dell' Opera del Duomo (Cathedral Works Museum) would have been part of the Duomo, if the plague of 1348 had not put an end to this massive project. Today it houses precious works of art from the Cathedral, including twelve 13th-century statues by Pisano, the superb Maestà *and the 26 Episodes of the* Passion *painted by Buoninsegna.*

The Museo Civico in the Palazzo Pubblico traces the political history of Siena.

The Sienese School of painting flourished in the 14th century with notable artists such as Simone Martini, Taddeo di Bartolo and the two Lorenzetti brothers. This artistic heritage is complemented by the superb buildings situated in the

On entering the town by the Camollia Gate, the visitor is welcomed by the motto 'Cor magis tibi sena pandit' (Siena opens its heart to you).

medieval heart of Siena. These are exceptional for their time in that they were constructed following a single architectural plan which was designed to create a veritable

The 49 feet (14 m) of frescoes of the Allegory of Good and Bad Government, *painted by Lorenzetti and completed in 1338, are one of the highlights of a visit to the Museo Civico.*

The Sienese Palio

The ritual of the Palio has taken place since the 14th century and is now held twice a year on July 2 and August 16. In a festive Renaissance setting, the 17 *contrade* (parishes) of Siena compete in a bareback horse race. Competitors set off on the slippery brick pavement and race around the piazza, encouraged by the shouting and yelling of crowds. The first horseman to make three circuits of the piazza is presented with a banner made of silk – the palio – bringing glory to his *contrada*...until the following year.

work of art. Nestling between the city's three hills, the bricks of the Piazza del Campo follow a natural dip in the ground to mark out a scallop-shaped square. Ever since the 14th century, the 'Palio', in homage to the Virgin, the patron saint of Siena, has taken place in this square, in front of the slightly concave façade of the **Palazzo Pubblico**. Completed in 1342, this building is one of the most beautiful Gothic monuments in Tuscany. The Torre del Mangia (built 1338–1348) towers 330 feet (102 metres) above the left wing of the palazzo that houses the Museo Civico.

In the Middle Ages, tall fortified houses such as these earned the town the name of San Gimignano dalle belle torri ('San Gimignano of the fine towers').

Tuscany: a relaxing setting in which to while away the hours.

San Gimignano
and the Chianti region

The fertile region of Tuscany enjoyed a surge in its fortunes during the Middle Ages, developing its commerce to sell crafts and produce from the land. The

The vines planted on the hills around San Gimignano produce the wines of Brunello di Montalcino, Chianti and Vernaccia. This dry white wine, with its slightly bitter after taste, is a perfect complement to the rabbit used in local recipes.

high towers of San Gimignano were built to protect the Chianti region.

The architecture of San Gimignano was intended to inspire fear.

Above: The fortified towers overlook a maze of rooftops and covered passages.

The town's many taverns provide a medieval setting in which to try finocchiona, a type of pork sausage flavoured with fennel seeds.

As you follow the course of the Elsa River from Siena, the high medieval towers of **San Gimignano** gradually come into view. The town's 14 fortified houses, together designated as a World Heritage Site by UNESCO, are the remnants of the 76 that were built in the 13th century. At that time, the city owed its prosperity to the dynamism of its merchants who profited from pilgrims passing through on their way to Rome.

In San Gimignano, the medieval skyscrapers are a spectacular sight, creating a distinctly theatrical setting.

In the Chianti region, the cultivation of the vine dates back to Etruscan times. The Etruscan people exported their wine as far away as Gaul.

A wine producing farm in the Vernaccia region, near San Gimignano.

At San Gimignano, each powerful family built a *casa torre* as a symbol of their wealth, aiming to make it taller than the one next door. Allied families even built aerial bridges between their houses. During the 14th century, the rivalries between the Guelph and Ghibelline factions, the terrible black death of 1348 and the diversion of the pilgrim route all weakened the city which eventually fell into Florentine hands.

In Chianti, the villages of Greve, Radda, Panzano, Castellina and Gaiole all have the right to produce the Chianti Classico wine. The bottles of these vineyards can be identified by the black cockerel on their labels.

In the villages built on the steep slopes of the mountainous islands of the Tuscan Archipelago, streets are replaced by flights of steps.

S outhern Tuscany can be divided into the mining region of the Colline Metallifere and the marshy coast of the Maremma.

Piombino in southern Tuscany.

Southern Tuscany

Massa Marittima celebrates the Balestro del Girifalco or 'Falcon Contest'.

The 24,700 acres (10,000 hectares) of dunes, pine groves, marshland and scrub of the Maremma Nature Reserve provide a habitat for migrating birds, as well as boars and badgers.

Since the Middle Ages, the town of **Massa Marittima** has profited from its location between the Marrema coastal region and a hinterland rich in ore. During the 14th century, the Sienese incorporated the town into the Republic of Siena in order to control the mining of lead, copper, iron and silver. This marked the start of the town's decline which was accelerated by epidemics of the plague and malaria. During the 19th century, the drainage of the marshes made the region healthier to live in and, along with industrial development, gave Massa Marittima a new lease of life.

The coastal resort of Castiglione della Pescaia has preserved its Tuscan charm.

For many years the **Maremma** was of little interest because of the mediocre quality of its marshy soil. Today, the drained area has become Tuscany's main beach, including the resorts of Follonica and Marina di Grossetto. To the south, a 9-mile (15-kilometre) strip of land preserved in its natural state forms the Parco Naturale dell'Uccellinal (Maremma Nature Reserve). The natural hot springs of Saturnia are also nearby.

The popular resort of Saturnia is also famous for its Roman and Etruscan remains.

Near the village of Saturnia, sulphurous springs reach a temperature of 99°F (37°C) in large natural pools.

127

Ships have docked at Portoferraio, capital of the island of Elba, since 1548.

In the upper part of Portoferraio, the P a l a z z i n a Napoleonica dei Mulini bears traces of Napoleon's stay, including the imperial eagle (left).

From the ports of Piombino and Porto Santo Stefano, boats offer excursions to the islands of Giglio, Montecristo, Elba and Capraia. Giglio attracts naturalists who come to study the wildlife, including the last Mediterranean mouflon (a wild mountain sheep). Montecristo, a hilly islet in the **Tyrrhenian Sea**, inspired the French author Alexandre Dumas to write the novel *The Count of Montecristo.*

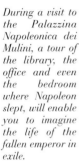

During a visit to the Palazzina Napoleonica dei Mulini, a tour of the library, the office and even the bedroom where Napoleon slept, will enable you to imagine the life of the fallen emperor in exile.

The island of **Elba**, the largest in the Tuscan Archipelago, has been famous since Roman times for its rich iron deposits. Its name is, in fact, derived from the Etruscan word *ilva* which means 'iron'. These deposits, combined with an extremely mild climate, attracted the interest of many powers. The island thus passed from Etruscan hands to the Carthaginians, then to the Romans, the Pisans, the Genoese, the Spanish, the Turks and the French. During the 16th century, Cosimo de' Medici built the new port of Portoferraio which was protected by an impressive citadel.

Napoleon's Exile

After his abdication on April 6, 1814, Napoleon was granted the rather derisory sovereignty of the island of Elba by the coalition that had just defeated France. The emperor settled in the port of Portoferraio, in a Medicean villa, known from then on as the Palazzina Napoleonica. He also owned a summer villa not far from the capital. Not satisfied with the tranquillity of the island, the fallen emperor escaped after a stay of just nine months, evading his English captors. Still entertaining dreams of conquering Europe, he returned to France where in 1815 he was defeated at the Battle of Waterloo and forced into exile again, this time on St Helena.

Creative Workshop

Having discovered the wonders of Florence and Tuscany, it's now time to get creative.

All you need are a few odds and ends and a little ingenuity to keep the spirit of your adventure alive by creating your own beautiful craft objects.

These simple yet ingenious ideas capture the special flavour of Florence and Tuscany and leave you with a permanent reminder of your visit.

An original, simple and fun way to preserve your holiday memories.

Millefiori Jewellery

*T*his ingenious use of Fimo polymer clay enable you to recreate brightly-coloured millefiori jewellery, popular in Italy in the 16th century.

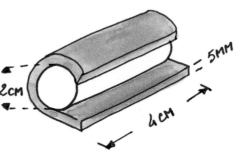

Modelling the Clay

• Knead one of the colours of Fimo polymer clay to soften it. Roll it to form a sausage 0.8" (2 cm) in diameter and 2" (5 cm) long. Using the roller, roll out some clay of a different colour into a strip 0.2" (5 mm) x 1.6" (4 cm) x 3.5" (9 cm). Surround the first sausage with this strip to form a new two-coloured sausage 2" (5cm) long and 1.8" (3cm) in diameter.

• Roll out two new colours of clay into a strip 0.16" (4mm) x 1.6" (4cm) x 2.75" (7cm). Place one of these strips on top of the other and roll them into a sausage.

• Repeat these processes so that you have one more sausage of each design. Keep two as they are and stretch the other two to a

length of about 1 foot (30cm).

Creating the Beads

• Cut each of the long sausages into six sections. Arrange these alternately around the fatter sausages.

Roll out this new sausage until smooth and until it is the diameter that you have decided to give each of your beads.

• Cut this sausage into long and short pieces. Make round beads by rolling the short pieces in your hands. Pierce the beads you intend to use for a necklace with a cocktail stick. Do not make a hole in the beads which you intend to make into earrings.

Baking the beads

• Place the beads on a sheet of aluminium foil on a baking tray and bake them for around 20 minutes at 266°F (130°C, gas mark 3/4). Let them cool before removing the cocktail sticks.

• String the beads or stick them on earring mountings.

Materials

• Fimo polymer clay in several colours (available from craft shops) • small roller made of hard rubber, normally sold with the polymer clay • wooden cocktail sticks • earring mountings • string for the necklace
• strong, fast-bonding glue for the earrings

Creating the outline

• Draw the landscape on a sheet of paper using a felt-tip pen, writing in the colour for each part of the tapestry. Centre the canvas on the drawing and trace the landscape with the felt-tip on to it.

Embroidering the picture

• Thread two strands of wool through the needle at a time. Most of the tapestry should be sewn using long stitches, six holes apart. These will need to be shorter in certain areas.

Tuscan Landscape Tapestry

T his beautiful tapestry recreates the undulating scenery of Tuscany. Its green valleys cascade down from a fairy-tale castle.

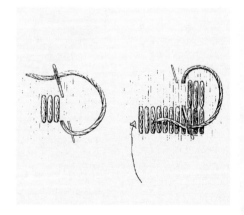

Mounting the picture

• When you have finished your embroidery, iron it with a warm iron on the reverse side. To keep your tapestry straight, back it with Bristol board before framing it.

• Centre the tapestry and fold the edges of the canvas over the Bristol board, pinning them together.

• With cotton and a large needle, sew the two ends of the canvas together proceeding from left to right, with long interlacing stitches. Remove the pins. Repeat the same process for the top and bottom.

The tapestry can now be framed.

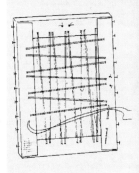

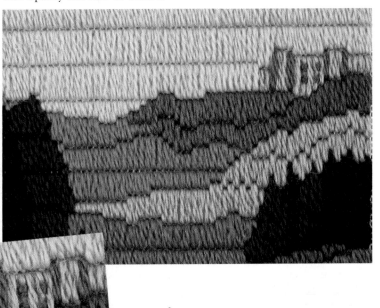

Materials

• tracing paper • tapestry canvas 9" x 12"(23 cm x 30 cm) • wool in a variety of colours: several different shades of green, including olive, khaki and bright green, beige, pink, brown, steel grey and blue
• marker pen with a fine tip and water-resistant ink
• size 22 tapestry needle • frame • Bristol board of slightly smaller dimensions than the frame • pins
• cotton or cord • large needle with a wide eye

*T*he Baptistry next to the Duomo in Florence boasts a beautiful traditional Tuscan tiled floor. Inspired by this floor, these white earthenware tiles have been painted with two of their patterns. Placed together, they make a novel mat for hot plates. Separately, they can be used as coasters.

Tile Table Mats

Making the stencil

• Copy the two designs suggested here, adjusting the size to fit your tiles using a photocopier. Cut out using a Stanley knife. Stick the stencil on the tiles using spray adhesive. One design should be able to create two tiles, since one is the negative of the other.

Painting the tiles

• Paint using black spray paint, or black enamel paint and a stencil brush. Carefully remove the stencil and allow to dry.

Materials

• 6 white earthenware tiles 6" x 6" (15 cm x 15 cm)
• ruler • Stanley knife • black pen • spray adhesive (of the type used for mounting photographs) • small pot of black enamel paint or can of black car spray paint
• stencil brush

Lipstick Case

*T*his lipstick case and mirror is decorated with the image of Botticelli's Venus.

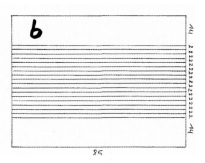

All measurements on the diagrams are in millimetres.

- Make one copy of diagram B and two of A on card. Make two copies of D on paper. Cut them out. With a Stanley knife, score B 18 times to produce grooves 0.08" (2mm) apart.
- Coat the rounded edges of A with water-based glue. Repeat on the reverse side of the very ends of the shorter sides of B. Stick the pieces together to form a U-shaped tube (Fig.1).
- Cover D with glue and stick on A, folding over the flaps (Fig. 2).

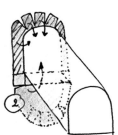

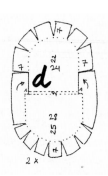

137

Making the flap

• Copy 'E' onto paper and cut it out.

•Apply a water-based glue to the hatched part of E and stick to the inside of the tube, folding the 0.4" (10mm) end section over on to the outside (Fig. 3).

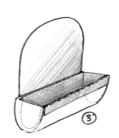

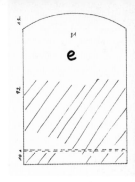

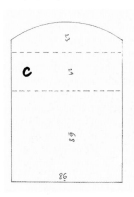

• Cut the piece marked 'C' out of Bristol board and the piece marked 'F' out of paper.

•Apply glue to F and Stick C to its centre. Fold the flaps over.

• Using a hammer, fix a press stud socket 0.6" (15mm) from the straight edge of F.

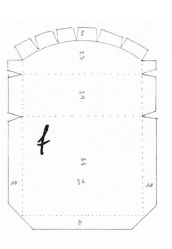

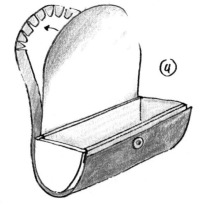

Attaching the cover

• Apply a water-based glue to 'C' and fold it around the tube, starting with the straight edge and working slowly round to the flap, folding over the edges (Fig. 4).

Adding the mirror

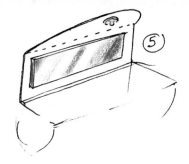

• Score along the lines of the two folds of the flap with the blunt edge of the Stanley knife and a ruler.
• Hammer on the press stud popper in line with its socket. Stick the mirror onto the inside of the flap (Fig. 5).

Decorating the case

• Make a colour photocopy of a postcard.
• Cut out your chosen picture or pattern and stick it over the case, scoring with the Stanley knife where the flap folds over.

Materials

• 0.04" (1mm) thick card • 200g Bristol board
• a sheet of 120g paper 8.3" x 11.7" (21 cm x 29.7 cm), 'elephant hide', 'marbled' or 'strata colour'
• metal ruler • Stanley knife • black pencil • stick of permanent glue • tube of water-based glue
• small mirror measuring 0.7" x 3" (18 mm x 76 mm) and 0.04" (1mm) thick • press stud and hammer

Tuscan Beans in Tomato Sauce

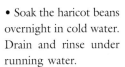

*F*or a simple meal with friends, try these haricot beans flavoured with tomatoes, garlic and olive oil. A taste of Tuscany brought to your table.

• Soak the haricot beans overnight in cold water. Drain and rinse under running water.

• Place them in a saucepan and cover them with cold water. Bring to the boil and cook for about a quarter of an hour. Strain.

• Peel the tomatoes and reduce them to a puree in the mixer or a puree seive. Strain the puree using a tea towel or a fine sieve.

• Pour the oil into a large saucepan, and add the finely chopped garlic and three sage leaves.

• Cook over a medium heat until the garlic turns brown.

• Add the haricots and tomato puree. Bring to the boil, then turn down the heat and simmer for 20 minutes.

• The haricots are cooked when the are still firm but slightly more crunchy. Test and season to taste.

• Place in a bowl, decorate with sage leaves and serve immediately.

Ingredients

To serve eight
• 18 oz (500g) dried haricot beans
• 14 oz (400g) well ripened tomatoes
• 3 cloves of garlic
• 4 tbsp olive oil
• Several fresh sage leaves
• Salt and pepper

INDEX

Acknowledgements

The publishers would like to thank all those who have contributed
to the preparation of this book, in particular:

Angie Allison, David Bême, Antoine Caron, Jean-Jacques Carreras,
Aude Desmortiers, Rupert Hasterok, Nicolas Lemaire, Hervé Levano,
Mike Mayor, Kha Luan Pham, Vincent Pompougnac,
Marie-Laure Ungemuth, Emmanuèle Zumstein.

Creative Workshop:
Michèle Forest (p. 132-133), Valérie Zuber (p. 136-137, 138-139)

Translation: Huw Jones.

Picture credits: Salamander Picture Library (p. 140-141).

Illustrations : Franz Rey, Valérie Zuber

Printed in Italy
Eurolitho – Milan
March 1999